Body in Motion

LITERACY network

MACMILLAN

CON

The Human Body at Work

MODULE 1

Page	Title	Genre	Comprehension Skill
4	**Pump Up the Heart** The human heart is a wondrous thing. What makes it tick? Read about this super-strong pump that keeps us alive.	Science Report	Cause and Effect
6	**Blood Banks** Have you ever wondered where blood is kept in case of emergencies? Find out about blood banks.	Information Report	Cause and Effect
10	**The Blood's Super Highway** Blood has a long way to travel each day. Discover where it goes and how it gets there.	Science Report	
12	**Breathe In, Breathe Out** Breathing is essential to life. Learn about how we breathe every day of our lives.	Science Report	
14	**The Silent Killer** Coronary Artery Disease (CAD) can cause heart attacks and even death. Understand how it works and how to prevent it.	Science Report	

Keeping the Body Working

MODULE 2

Page	Title	Genre	Comprehension Skill
16	**Radio 4LLL – Organ Donation** Twins Benjamin and Jamie talk about their organ donation operation to a radio talkshow host.	Discussion (Interview)	Fact and Opinion
18	**Stem Cell Research - The Great Debate** Hear from both sides of the argument about this current science debate.	Discussion	Fact and Opinion
22	**Give Blood!** Discover how to give blood and why blood donation is so important.	Exposition (Magazine Article)	
24	**Hospital Calls for Compulsory Organ Donation** Should organ donation be made compulsory? Read about the different opinions.	Discussion (Newspaper Article)	

TENTS

What Sorts of Things Affect My Body?

MODULE 3

		Genre
28	**Asthma** Find out about this common illness, its symptoms and treatments.	Explanation
30	**Allergy Versus Intolerance** Some people have reactions to certain foods or substances. It may be an allergy or intolerance. Find out the difference.	Explanation
34	**A-Choo!** Do you know what the most common substances are that cause allergies? Read about them here.	Explanation
36	**Anaphylactic Shock** Discover what happens to people who have life-threatening allergic reactions.	Explanation

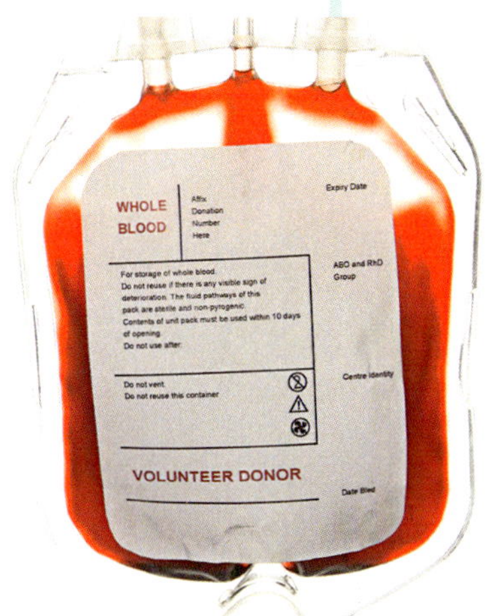

Regular Features

		Genre
40	**Get with the Beat** Learn how to find your heart rates at rest and after exercise. Take your pulse and discuss the results.	Procedure
42	**Mad about Health** A rap about staying in shape.	Poetry
44	**Mighty Marvel Muscle Meter** See how readers responded to an advertisement for a new fitness invention.	Persuasive Text
46	**Funtastic Human Body** Fun activities relating to the human body.	Puzzles and Games

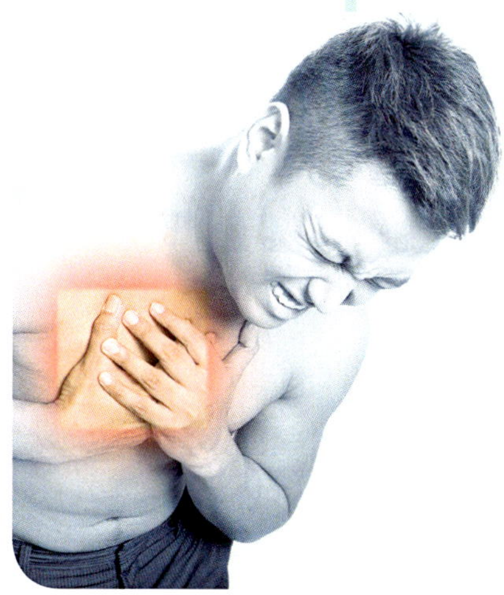

A = Assessment Text

Pump Up the Heart

What do you think of when you hear the word **heart**?

This is what a human heart looks like.

A human heart is made of super-strong muscle. In fact, it is the strongest muscle in a person's body! It needs to be strong because it has a very important job to do – pumping blood around the body. A heart pumps blood from a person's head to a person's toes through blood vessels called arteries, veins and capillaries. A heart works hard 24 hours a day – it never stops beating, otherwise the person would die!

Take a Look Inside

To find out the size of your heart, clench your hand into a fist. Your heart is the same size as your clenched fist.

As you grow bigger, your heart will grow larger, too. A human heart has four chambers – two on the left and two on the right. The two smaller chambers are called atriums, and the two larger chambers are called ventricles.

A heart works like a pump, as it squeezes and relaxes to push blood out of the heart and around a person's body. It is attached to veins and arteries. Blood flows into a heart through veins and away from a heart through arteries.

Pump Action

A heart fills with blood, then the muscle walls squeeze, or contract, then the blood is pushed out to the body. When a heart relaxes, it fills with blood again. Consequently, blood is pushed out to every single cell in a person's body.

Fun Fact

A human heart is a super-strong pump. A single squeeze could shoot water almost 2 metres into the air!

Fun Fact

A child's heart beats about 90 times a minute. An adult's heart beats about 70 times a minute. So, in one day, a person's heart can beat over 100,000 times!

Inside the Human Heart

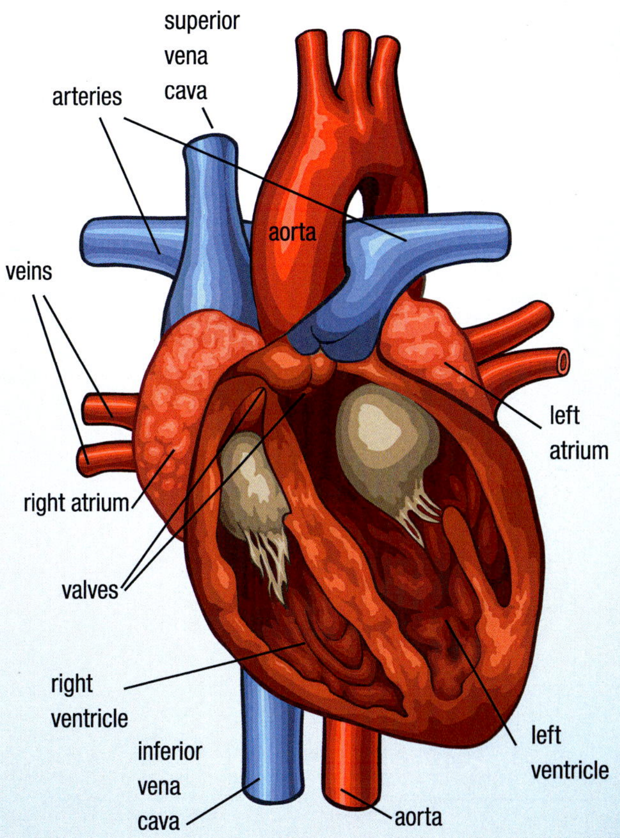

The Heart in Action

The beat you feel when you touch your wrist is the blood being pumped around your body, or your pulse.

A heart pumps blood around a person's body over and over in a cycle. One side of the heart takes blood filled with oxygen and nutrients and pumps it to different parts of the body. The other side takes the used blood from the body and pumps it to the lungs.

Left Side

Blood that has oxygen, or oxygenated blood, comes from the lungs, and it fills the left atrium.

The muscle walls contract, and this forces a valve to open and blood to gush into the left ventricle.

When the left ventricle is filled with blood, the valve closes and the walls contract. This opens another valve and the blood is squeezed through an artery to different parts of the body.

In the body, the blood picks up wastes such as carbon dioxide, and drops off oxygen and nutrients to the cells.

The blood then returns through veins to the right side of the heart to begin another cycle.

Right Side

Blood that has no oxygen, or deoxygenated blood, comes from the body, and this fills the right atrium.

The muscle walls contract, and this forces a valve to open and blood to gush into the right ventricle.

When the right ventricle is filled with blood, the valve closes and the walls contract. This opens another valve and the blood is squeezed through an artery to the lungs.

At the lungs, the blood picks up oxygen and becomes oxygenated, dropping off wastes such as carbon dioxide. The blood then returns through veins to the left side of the heart to begin another cycle.

BLOOD BANKS

Blood Basics

People cannot live without blood! Blood is the human body's main transportation system. It carries hundreds of vital substances to and from all the body's cells. Blood delivers food and oxygen to the body's cells, so they can function. It transports carbon dioxide and other waste products away from the cells. It helps protect a person from infection and disease. It even keeps a person's body at a safe temperature. All of these processes keep a person alive and healthy.

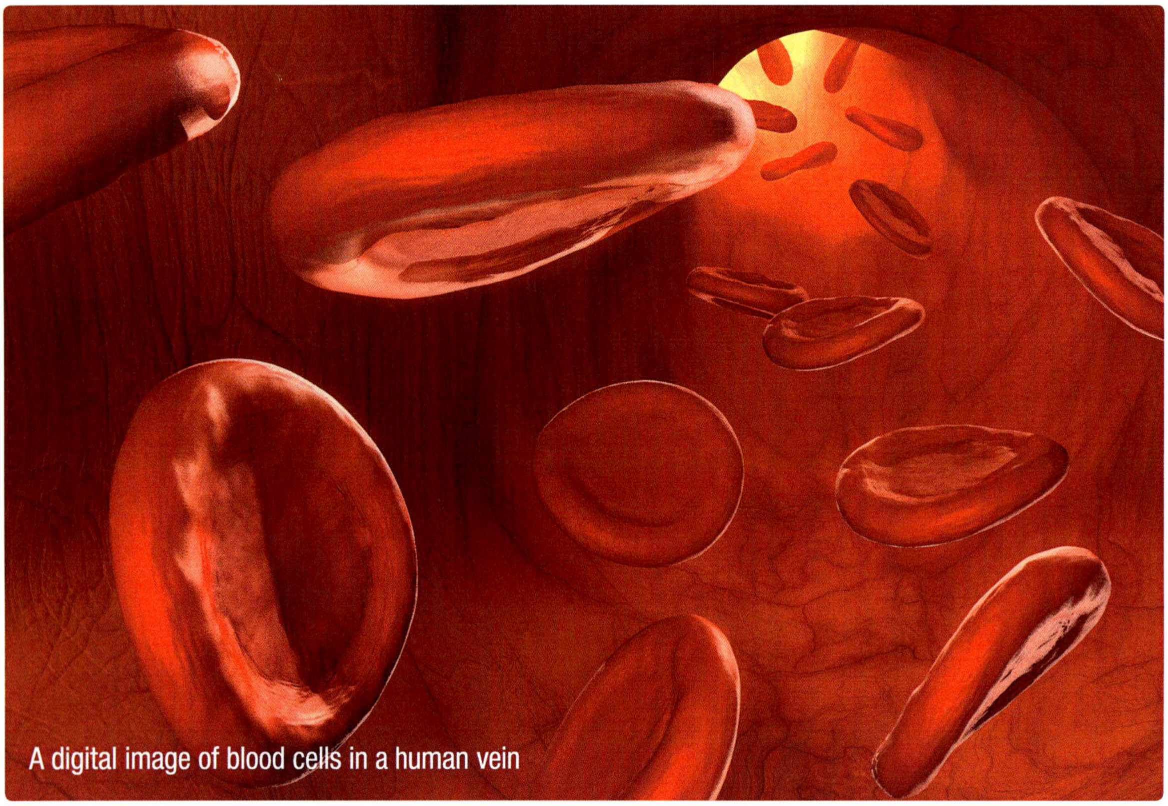

A digital image of blood cells in a human vein

An average adult has about 5 to 6 litres of blood. If a healthy person gets a minor cut, they could lose about half a litre and it would cause no ill effects at all. The person would be OK because the human body is designed so that it can lose some blood and replace it quite quickly. If a person loses more blood than their body can replace, they can become seriously ill or die.

Blood being stored at a blood bank

New Blood – FAST!

If a person loses too much blood, they will need to replace it with new blood quickly. To solve this problem, they can have another person's blood transferred directly into their bloodstream. This is called a blood transfusion. It could save the person's life.

To perform blood transfusions, hospitals need to have access to a clean and healthy supply of fresh blood. They get their supplies from a blood bank. A blood bank collects, stores and distributes blood. It works in a similar way to a regular money bank. In the same way that people deposit money until they need to withdraw it, healthy people can deposit blood. Then, people who need the blood can withdraw it later.

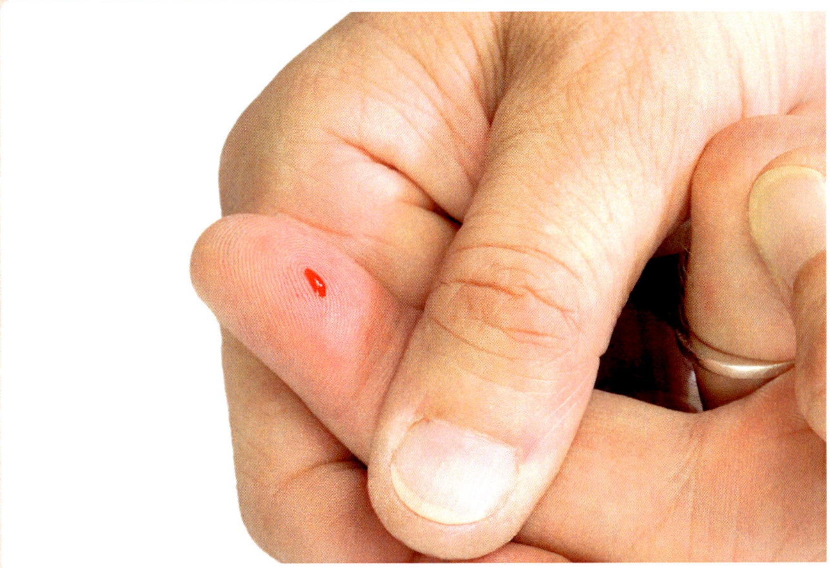

This is a minor cut.

The blood from blood banks is used to save many lives every year. However, blood needs to be used within a certain time period – before it goes off. Therefore, blood banks constantly need fresh blood to replenish their supplies. To do this, they ask healthy people to donate blood at a blood centre.

Deposits

A blood bank technician working with a blood donor in a portable bloodmobile

People who deposit their blood into a blood bank are called donors. To donate blood, donors need to be aged between 16 and 70 years, be in good health and weigh more than 45 kilograms. Before a donation is taken, the donor must fill in a questionnaire. This is to ensure that their blood is suitable and that they are not endangering their own health by giving blood.

The blood is taken by putting a needle into the donor's arm. In about 5–10 minutes, almost half a litre of their blood is collected. This does not harm the donor, because the donor's body can quickly replace the blood. After giving blood, a healthy donor must wait three months before donating blood again. As a result, the donor will never lose too much of their own blood.

At the Bank

It is important to make sure that the donated blood supply at the blood bank is safe. Therefore, the blood is tested to make sure it does not carry any diseases. If it did carry diseases, these could be transferred into the person who receives the blood. It could make them very sick.

People have different blood types, so not everyone can use the same sort of donated blood. If a person received the wrong blood type, it could make them even sicker, so it is important that the blood is sorted into the correct blood types. It is also important that blood banks have adequate supplies of all the different blood types, so that no one misses getting the blood they need.

Withdrawals

If a person is in an accident, or has surgery, they may lose a lot of blood and need blood from a blood bank.

But, the blood from a blood bank is used in many other ways, too. For example, it is used for medical research and for cancer patients.

A whole blood donation is separated into three components. It is divided into platelets, plasma and red blood cells. This makes it possible for just one donation to save the lives of up to three people.

When you consider just how much can be done with half a litre of blood, it is easy to see why blood banks are a vital part of today's society.

A technician may handle blood donations in test tubes.

How Red Blood Cells Are Used

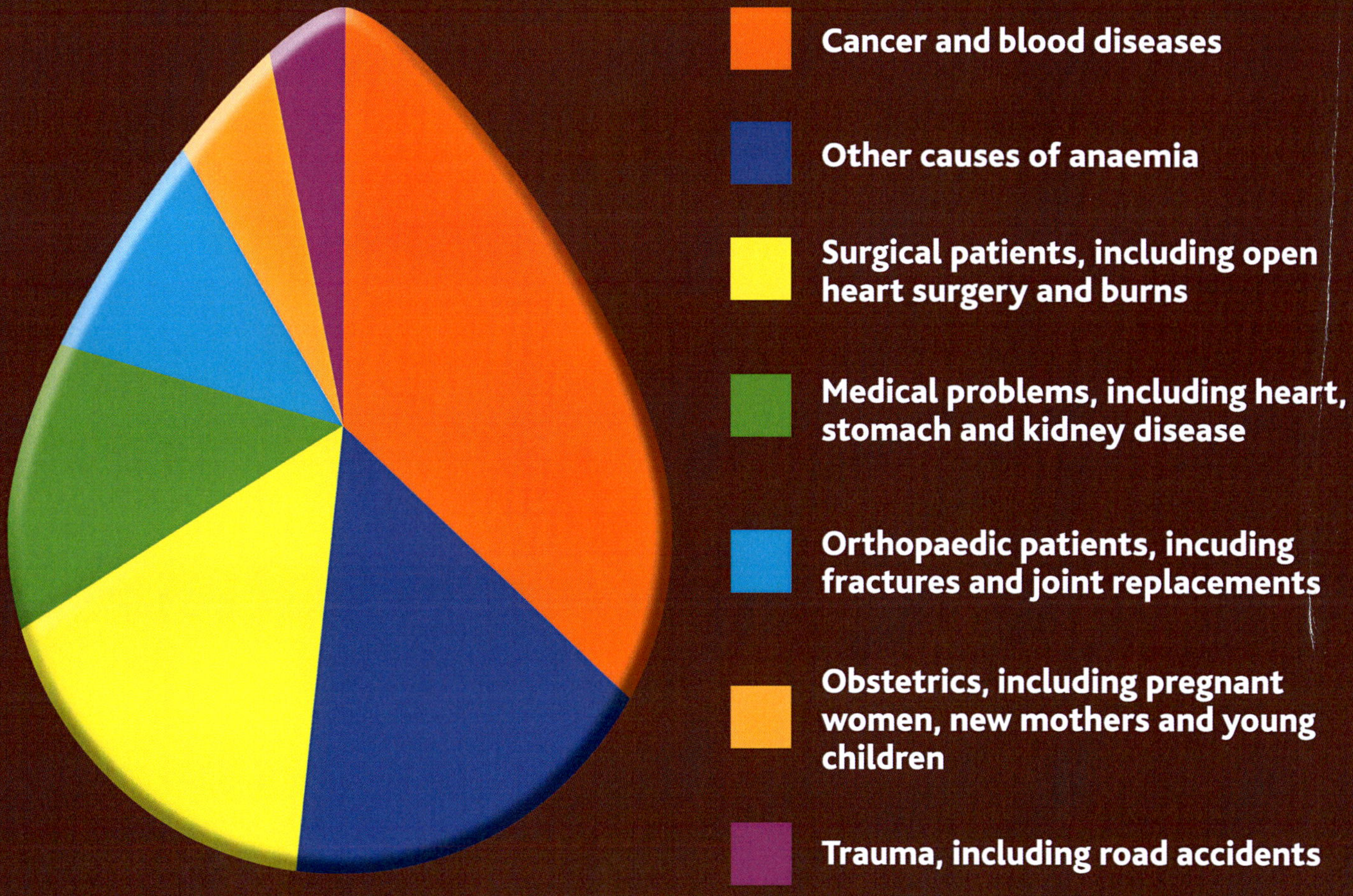

The Blood's Super Highway

Each day, your blood circles your body over and over. On its journey, your blood travels through a vast network of tubes called blood vessels. There are three kinds of blood vessels – arteries, capillaries and veins.

Arteries

Arteries are the blood vessels through which blood is pumped away from the heart.

Oxygenated blood begins its journey in the largest artery, called the aorta. The aorta then branches into smaller arteries through which blood is pumped to the various parts of the body.

Arteries need to be strong because the blood being pumped by the heart is under high pressure. Arteries need to be flexible, or elastic, to expand and make room for the blood that is being forced into them. The arterial walls contract, squeezing the blood further along the artery. This keeps the blood circulating through the body. Smaller arteries continue to branch off the main arteries until they feed into the next stage of the journey – the capillaries.

Capillaries

Capillaries connect the smallest arteries to the smallest veins and are the blood's loading and unloading zones. Unlike arteries, capillaries have super-thin walls. Oxygen and nutrients from the blood can easily pass through the capillary walls and into the cells of the tissues.

Facts

- If an artery is cut, blood gushes out in spurts as the heart beats.
- The blood carried by most arteries is bright red because it is oxygenated.
- Each heartbeat pumps about five tablespoons, or 70 millilitres, of blood into your arteries.

Waste materials, such as carbon dioxide, can pass from the cells into the blood. Once the pick-ups and deliveries are complete, the blood travels to the next kind of blood vessels, called the veins.

Veins

Veins are the blood vessels that carry blood back to the heart.

At first, the capillaries feed into tiny veins. These small veins then join together to form larger ones, again and again, until all of the returning blood finally arrives back at the heart.

Blood that is returning from the head and arms feeds into the heart through the superior vena cava vein. Blood that is returning from the trunk and legs feeds into the heart through the inferior vena cava vein. From here, the blood is pumped to the lungs where it drops off its waste products and picks up fresh oxygen. It is then pumped back to the heart through the pulmonary veins. The blood is now ready to begin its journey through the body again!

Facts

- Capillaries are the smallest blood vessels in the body. In fact, most capillaries are so small that only one blood cell can pass through them at a time!

The Circulatory System

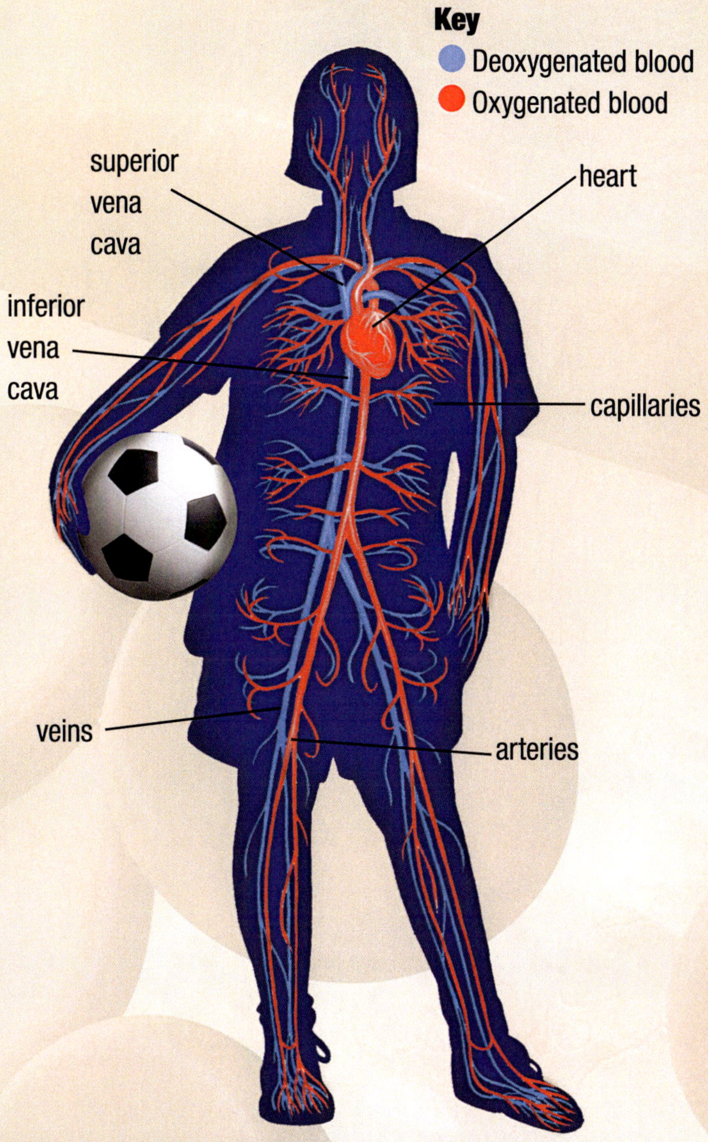

Blood Flow to and From the Heart

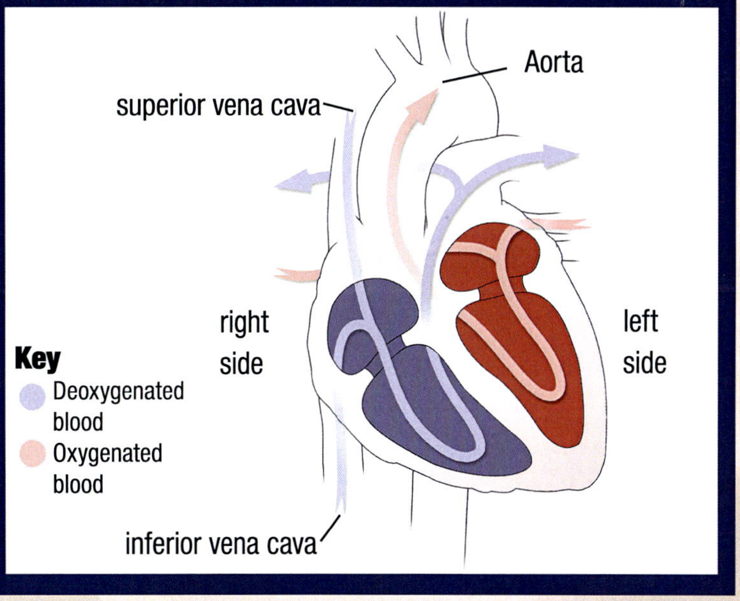

The right side of the heart deals with deoxygenated blood, while the left side deals with oxygenated blood.

Breathe In, *Breathe Out*

Take a deep breath – you've just sucked in about half a litre of air. Did you notice your chest expand? Where did all that air go? The answer is – your lungs.

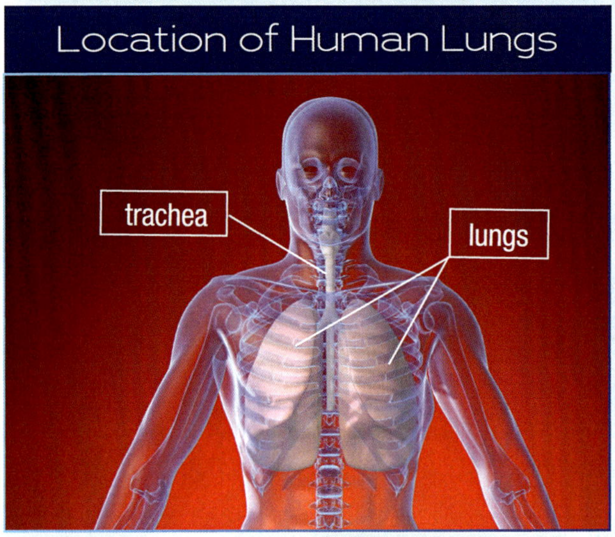

Lungs are the body's one-stop shop for gas exchange. Every single cell in the human body needs oxygen for energy. A person gets the oxygen from the air around them. They breathe the air into their lungs. Then, it is the job of the lungs to get the oxygen into the bloodstream, so the heart can pump it to the cells.

As the blood drops off oxygen, it picks up waste gases, such as carbon dioxide. The heart pumps the blood carrying the carbon dioxide back to the lungs. Then, the lungs get the carbon dioxide out of the body. Basically, the lungs, heart and blood work together to exchange the good gas for the bad.

A person has two lungs – a left lung and a right lung.

When a person takes a deep breath, air rushes into their nose and down their windpipe, or trachea. From there, it flows down two tubes into the lungs. These tubes are called bronchi. One goes to the right lung, while the other goes to the left lung.

The air then rushes into thousands of tiny tubes branching off the bronchi. These tubes are called bronchioles.

Finally, the air reaches a cluster of tiny air sacs called alveoli. Each of these alveoli is covered with a net of tiny blood vessels. The walls of these blood vessels are so thin that gases pass through easily. The oxygen passes from the alveoli into the blood. The carbon dioxide passes from the blood into the alveoli.

Then, as a person breathes back out, the stale air rushes back up all of the tubes and out the person's nose.

Parts of the Human Lungs

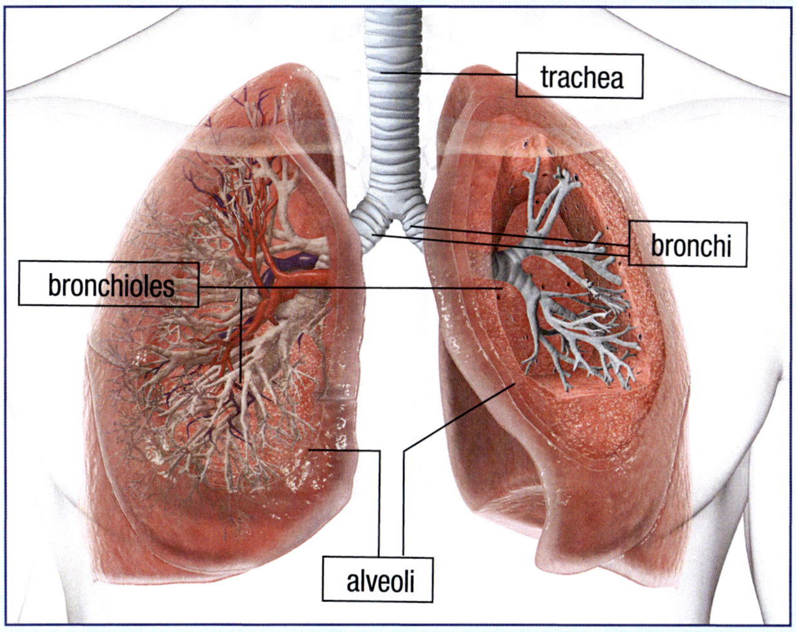

A person breathes about 15 times every minute and they don't even have to think about it!

This is because breathing is controlled by the body's nervous system. Nerves carry impulses from parts of the brain to the lungs to make them work automatically. Even if a person tries to hold their breath, their brain forces them to breathe.

Watch Out – Invaders!

The air is teeming with bacteria, viruses, dust and pollutants. With each breath, these make their way straight into a person's lungs. To combat this, lungs have a built-in protection system. The tubes inside the lungs are lined with a sticky fluid called mucus.

Many of the harmful invaders are trapped in the mucus. The mucus and captives are then pushed up into the throat by tiny hairlike structures called cilia. Then, they are coughed up or swallowed. Special cells in the alveoli destroy any harmful substances that get through this first line of defence.

It is important that a person looks after their lungs, because they cannot live without them! One way a person can look after their lungs is by exercising.

When a person exercises, they have to breathe harder to get more oxygen to their cells. As they breathe more deeply, and take in more air, their lungs become stronger.

The Silent Killer

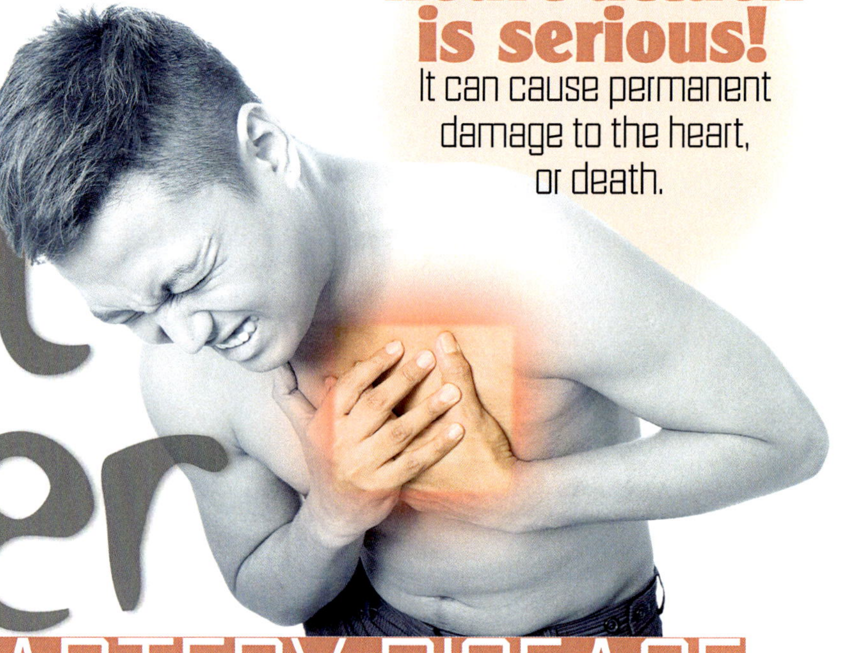

A heart attack is serious! It can cause permanent damage to the heart, or death.

CORONARY ARTERY DISEASE

What Is Coronary Artery Disease (CAD)?

Coronary artery disease (CAD) is one of the most common forms of heart disease and a leading cause of heart attacks.

The coronary arteries carry blood to supply the heart with the oxygen and nutrients it needs to keep pumping. CAD occurs when deposits of fat and calcium build up on the interior walls of these arteries, causing them to harden and thicken. These deposits are called plaque. As the plaque builds up, it narrows the arteries and restricts the flow of blood to the heart.

As a result, the heart does not get enough oxygen and nutrients to do its work. This can damage the heart and possibly lead to a heart attack.

What Is a Heart Attack?

If an artery becomes completely blocked, the blood supply to part of the heart is cut off. This can cause some of the heart muscle to die, damaging the heart.

A complete blockage usually begins when some of the plaque cracks. This causes a collection of blood cells, and other parts of the blood, to form a clot over the damaged area. This suddenly blocks the blood flow to part of the heart muscle and causes a heart attack.

What Causes CAD?

There are many conditions and day-to-day habits that can lead to CAD. These are some of them:

- It can be caused by genetics and be passed from one family generation to the next.
- It can be caused by a high amount of a fatty substance called cholesterol in the blood. This is because the cholesterol adds to the plaque and narrows the walls of the coronary arteries.
- It can be caused by high blood pressure. This is because high blood pressure forces the heart to work harder. If the heart is working harder, it needs more blood through the coronary arteries.
- It can be caused by conditions such as diabetes, stress and obesity.

How Can I Avoid Coronary Artery Disease?

CAD builds up over time. Some influencing factors, such as age, gender and genetics can't be helped, but there are some simple things that you can do to lower your risk of CAD.

By following these simple tasks, you can keep a healthy body weight and strengthen your heart. You can also lower your cholesterol and blood pressure. You can lower your chances of getting CAD!

Eat a healthy, well-balanced diet

Exercise regularly

Be smoke-free

Radio 4LLL

www.radio4lllmorningshow.com.au

Organ Donation

Radio 4LLL
Music – News
Interviews

Home | Listen | What's On | Music | Podcasts

Radio Interview Transcript
23 December 2008

Presenter: Katarina Clark

Katarina Clark: Good morning, this is Katarina Clark for Radio 4LLL. This morning I'm at Metropolis Hospital to interview two remarkable young men, twin brothers Benjamin and Jamie. A few days ago, both Benjamin and Jamie had major operations. Jamie was sick, but Benjamin was perfectly healthy. It's a bit unusual to have an operation when you're healthy, so let's find out about it. Benjamin and Jamie, how are you feeling now?

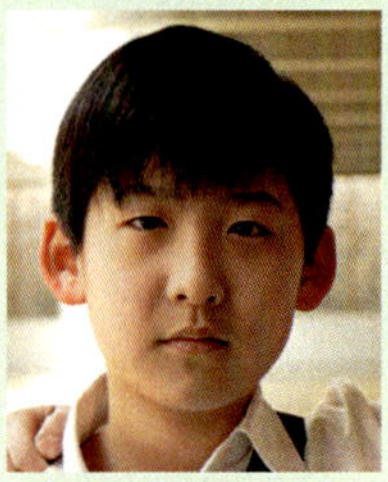

Benjamin: Not bad, thanks.

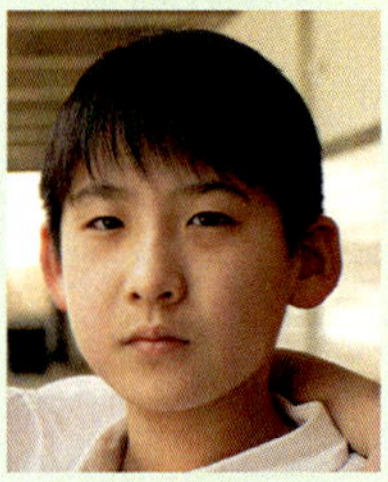

Jamie: A bit sore, but I feel a lot better than I did before the operation!

Katarina Clark: So, what was the operation for?

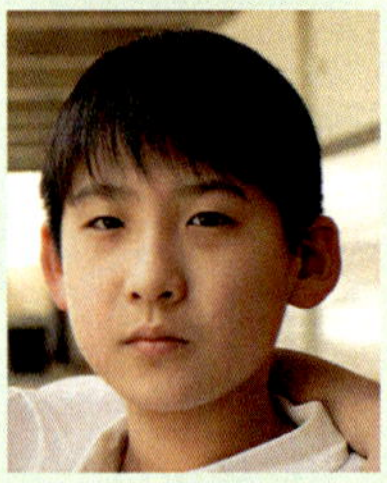

Jamie: It was a life-saving kidney transplant. I've been sick for years, and my kidneys weren't cleaning my blood like they were meant to. I spent a lot of time in hospital on a dialysis machine that cleaned my blood, but it wasn't fixing my kidneys. Benjamin donated one of his kidneys to me.

Radio 4LLL

www.radio4lllmorningshow.com.au

Katarina Clark: A kidney is a very generous gift, Benjamin. Surely Jamie could have waited for a donor organ?

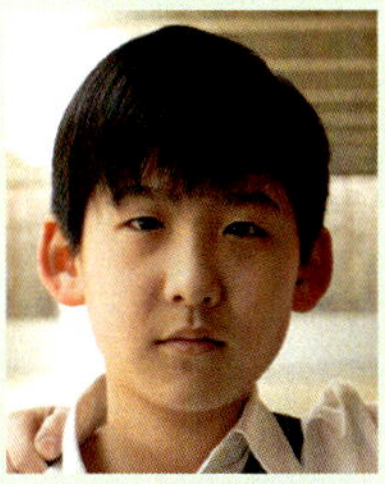

Benjamin: There are more than 1,800 people on waiting lists for organ transplants in Australia. About 75 per cent of these people are waiting for kidneys. Sadly, some of these people will die waiting, because there are not enough donor organs. I didn't want Jamie to die, so I gave him one of my kidneys.

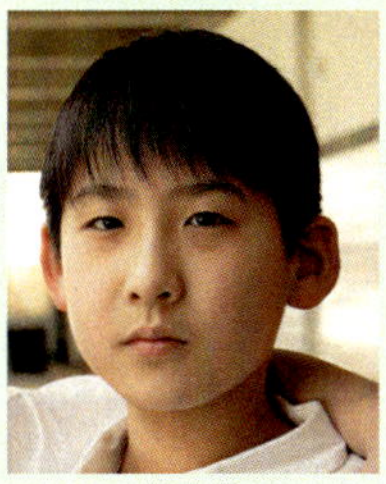

Jamie: I think everyone should consider being on Australia's Organ Donor Register. Thousands of people could live healthier lives if others were prepared to donate their organs when they die.

Katarina Clark: Or even when they're alive, like Benjamin! However, there are some scary facts about organ donation. In some countries, they use organs from executed prisoners for transplants. I've heard that some prisoners don't get fair trials, because the demand for organs is so high.

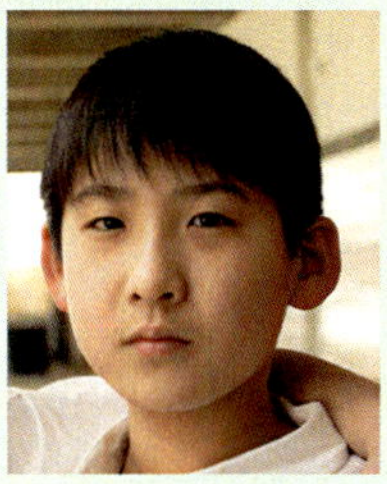

Jamie: I don't know if that's true. But, I do know that in some countries people can sell one of their kidneys. If a person is poor, then it is a good way for them to get money. I heard that about 100 people in India sold their kidneys after a tsunami destroyed the fishing grounds and they had no income. Perhaps it saved their families.

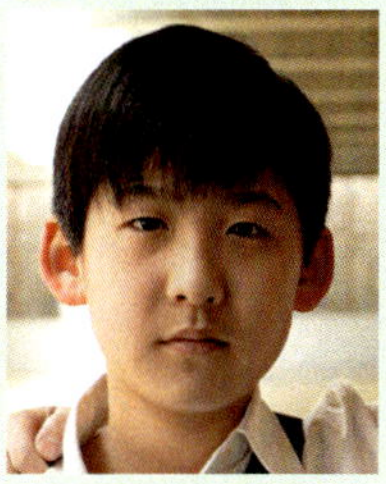

Benjamin: Well, I'm not so sure that I'd say it was a good way to get money. It's a major operation! Besides, I think that allowing people to sell one of their kidneys can lead to problems. It pressures poorer people into doing something that they don't really want to do. Some people believe that adults and children have been kidnapped by criminals and had their organs stolen and sold.

Katarina Clark: Well, it's clear there are arguments for and against organ donation. This kidney transplant has had a very happy outcome, though. Thanks Benjamin and Jamie – it's good to see you both looking so well.

Podcast

STEM CELL RESEARCH – THE GREAT DEBATE

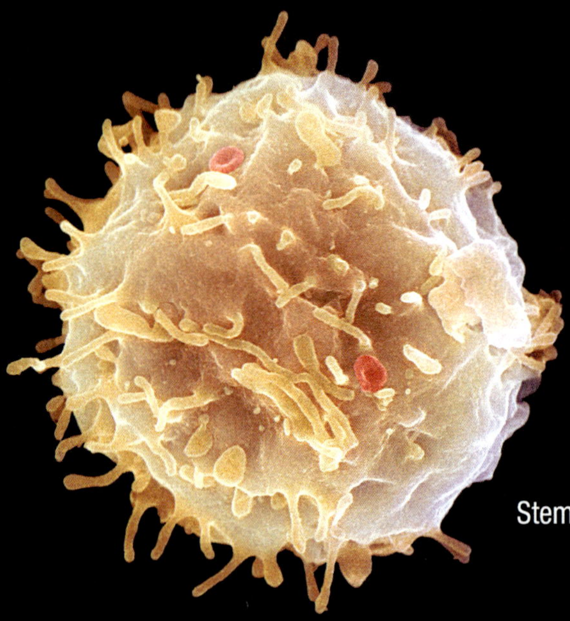

Stem cell

As soon as a tiny human egg is fertilised, it becomes a factory of rapidly multiplying cells. It becomes known as an embryo and is destined to grow and develop into a human baby. After five days, an embryo is still smaller than the full stop at the end of this sentence. However, it is busy producing some very special cells – stem cells. These cells are special because, in the right environment, they can grow into any kind of body cell.

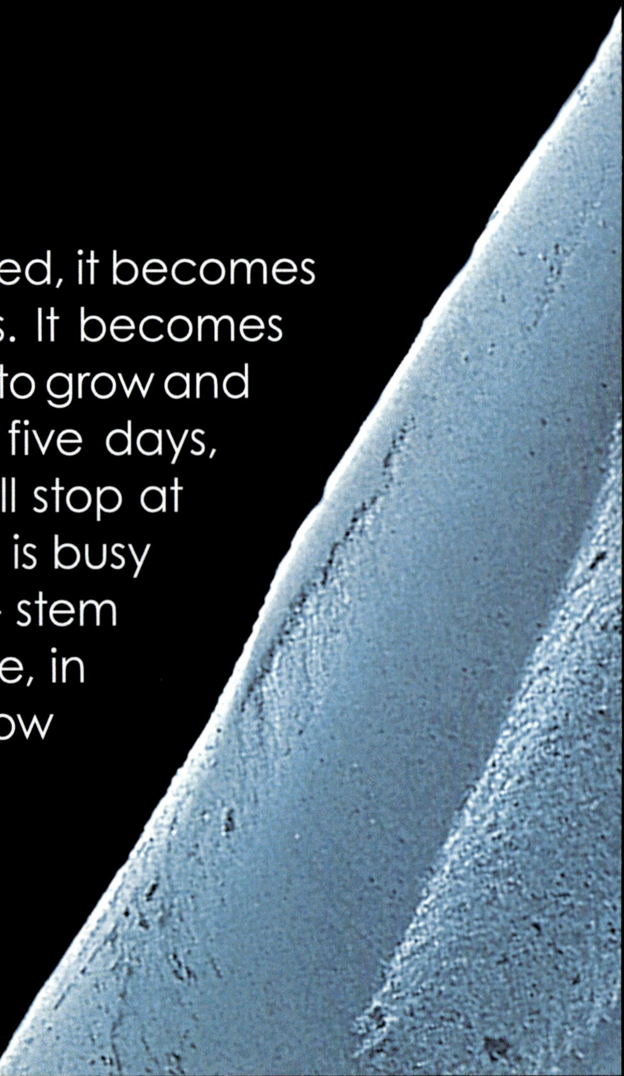

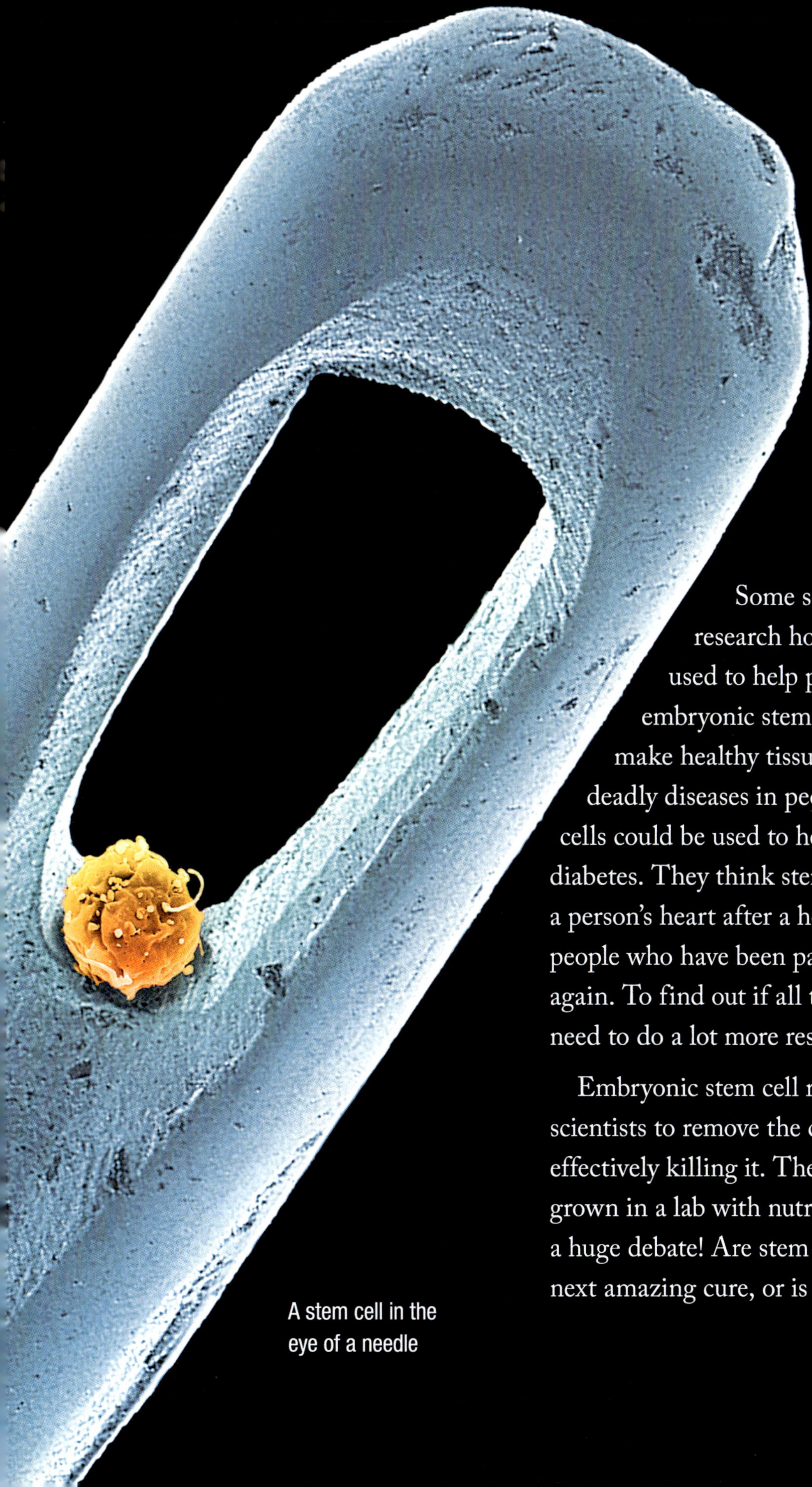

Some scientists would like to research how these cells can be used to help people. They believe that embryonic stem cells could be used to make healthy tissues and organs to cure deadly diseases in people. They hope stem cells could be used to help people who have diabetes. They think stem cells could help repair a person's heart after a heart attack, or give people who have been paralysed a chance to walk again. To find out if all this is possible, scientists need to do a lot more research.

Embryonic stem cell research requires scientists to remove the cells from an embryo, effectively killing it. The stem cells are then grown in a lab with nutrients. This has sparked a huge debate! Are stem cells destined to be the next amazing cure, or is science going too far?

A stem cell in the eye of a needle

My sister is very sick. She has a disease in a large organ in her abdomen, her liver. She might die. If more research had been done on embryonic stem cells, doctors would probably be able to cure her by now. I definitely think scientists should be allowed to research embryonic stem cells. The five-day old embryos that they use are just a bundle of cells. They don't have a nervous system, or any identifying features. The research would benefit many people in the future. I'm sure it would save my sister's life!

The whole idea of embryonic stem cell research makes me sad and angry. It is immoral to kill human embryos in the name of science. It is only a matter of time before the cells in an embryo become a human baby. Therefore, it is like killing a baby. Remember, you were once an embryo, too!

I can't believe people are so upset about using embryos for research. Most of the embryos are donated by fertility clinics. These embryos would be destroyed anyway. It is immoral to throw away these valuable cells when they could be used to save a person's life!

The research is just the start. If there is a breakthrough in the research, then millions of embryos will be needed to save all the sick people in the world. Where will all these embryos come from? There will be embryo farms everywhere! If people put aside their morals for this research, it will make it okay for scientists to do other terrible research in the future.

Scientists who are researching embryonic stem cells experiment on animals. For example, rats are hurt so they can't use their back legs. Then they're injected with stem cells to fix their spinal chords. This is cruel.

It is important that scientists experiment on animals first, so they can make sure it is safe to use stem cell therapies on humans. Surely if it is going to help so many people, a few mice is a small sacrifice. After all, millions of people catch and kill mice in their homes every year.

The government in my country is against embryonic stem cell research. But, many other countries around the world are doing a lot of research. Some of our great scientists have moved to other countries so they can work there. If we don't keep up with the rest of the world, we will end up behind in science.

GIVE BLOOD!

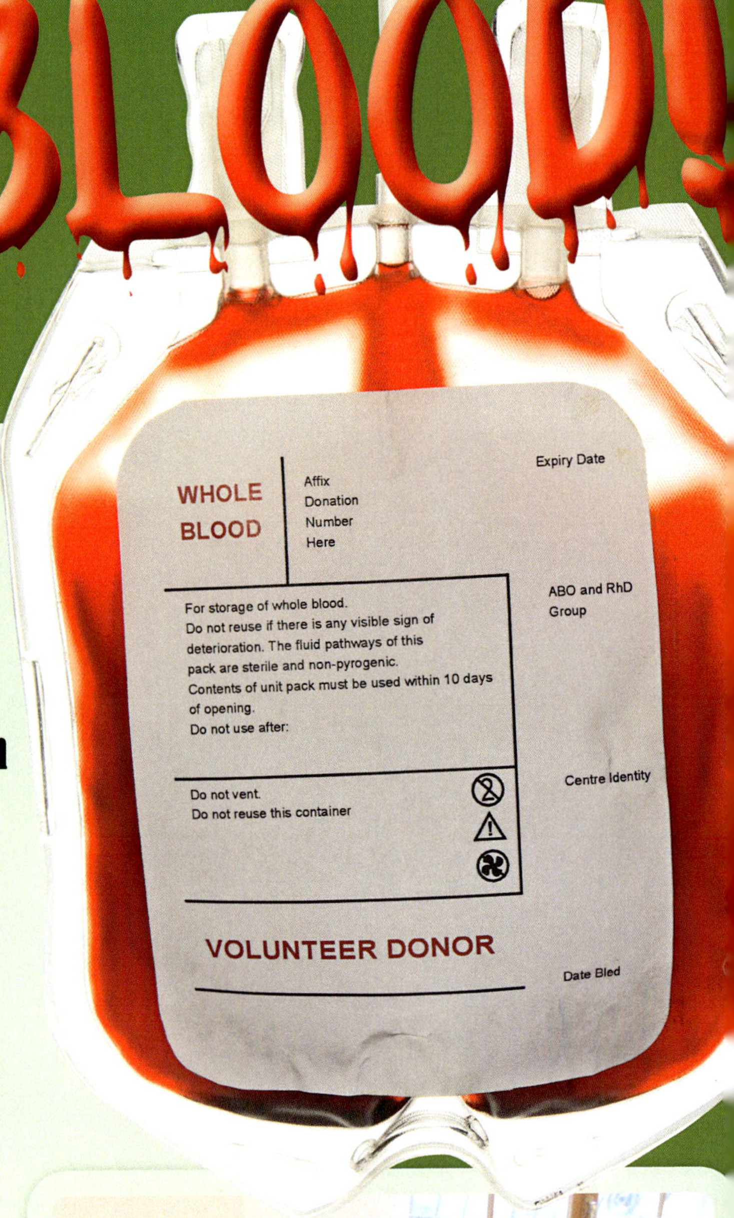

Someone, somewhere in the world, urgently needs blood. If they don't get it right now, they are going to die! All it would take to save their life is half a litre of your blood. Could you look them in the eye and tell them you wouldn't give them the gift of life?

Blood banks depend on healthy people to donate blood. While many people roll up their sleeves and give generously, it is not enough. Blood supplies in blood banks around the world are nearly always on the verge of running out. If giving blood is made compulsory for all healthy people, then blood banks will always have a steady supply. Many more lives could be saved!

Who Needs Blood?

The list of people who need blood is long. Accident victims, surgery patients and people with diseases, such as cancer and anaemia, all need blood. But, only a small fraction of people who are able to donate, actually do. Most people are unaware of the huge difference their blood can make. A single donation can save the lives of up to three people.

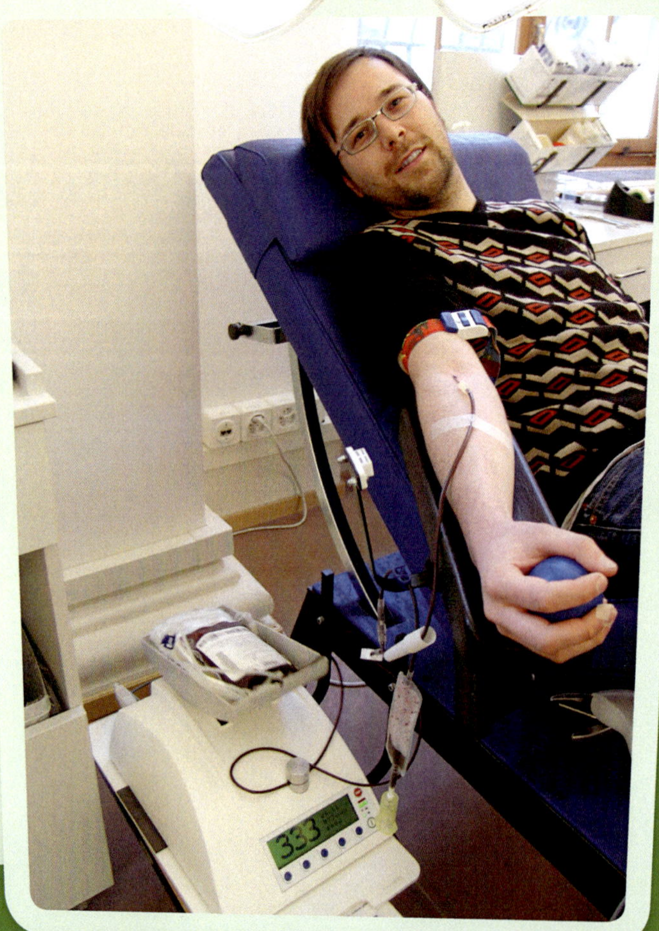

A man giving blood

Meet Arana

Arana is four years old. She loves kittens and drawing. She has a blood disorder and needs regular blood transfusions, or she would get sick and die. Every year, Arana depends on 24 donors to provide enough blood for her transfusions.

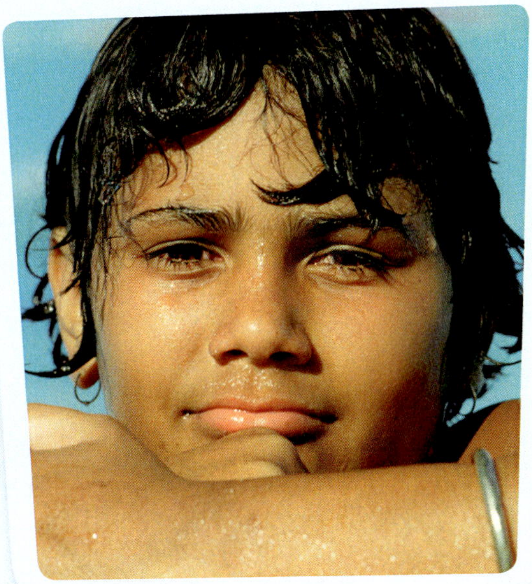

Meet Billy

Billy is 10 years old and his favourite sport is Aussie Rules. Last year, Billy was diagnosed with a type of cancer called leukaemia. So far, he has received 26 units of blood and 18 units of platelets. His treatment is now working – Billy has a chance at a normal healthy life.

Meet Mei

Mei has two young children. Last summer, she was in a car accident. She lost a lot of blood from her injuries. When Mei arrived at the hospital, she was given a blood transfusion that saved her life. Mei is grateful that she now has the chance to watch her children grow up.

Healthy people like you and me are the only source of this life-saving blood. If it were compulsory for people to donate blood, then there would be life-saving blood for everyone, all the time.

All it takes is half an hour out of your day. You can make a difference. So, sign our petition to make it compulsory to donate blood, and save a life or three!

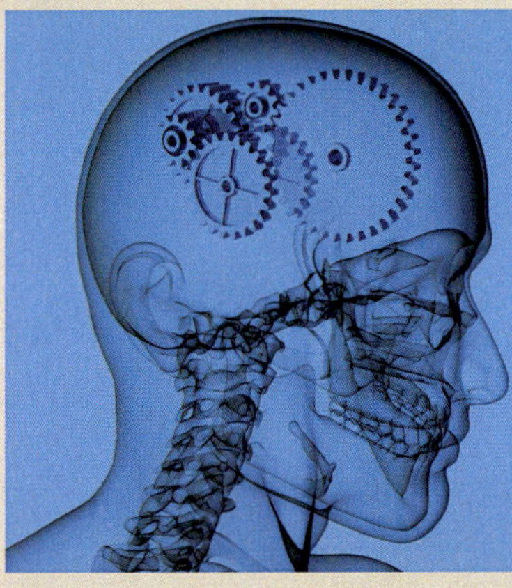

Health Debates WEEKLY

Hospital Calls for Compulsory Organ Donation

March 2007

'It's time to make organ donation compulsory!' This is the call from one of the country's leading hospitals, Grand Western in Victoria. They want to battle the shortage of organs needed for organ transplant operations.

During the hospital's annual meeting, several doctors announced their intention to launch a campaign to change the organ donation law. They plan to lobby politicians to change the existing voluntary organ donation system to an opt-out system. 'We have the skills to perform organ transplant operations. We can transplant lungs, livers and hearts. We can even transplant part of a person's intestines or pancreas. Every year, thousands of people die needlessly because there aren't enough donor organs,' stated Doctor Munroe.

Doctor Munroe, Grand Western Hospital, VIC

Under the current voluntary system, if a person is willing to donate their organs, they have to register on a donor list. Then, they carry an organ donor card. In the event of the person's death, doctors still have to get permission from the patient's family members before removing the organs. Doctors claim this system is not working. There are not enough organs being donated. Under the new opt-out system, people would be registered on the donor list from birth. If a person doesn't want to donate their organs, they can complete a form to have their name removed from the list. They can opt out.

'We are not saying that everyone has to donate their organs. We're just changing the system to make it work better. The opt-out policy would save thousands of lives,' said Munroe. 'It would also save family members the distress of having to be asked about organ donation.'

Some countries have already introduced the opt-out policy. They are seeing a significant improvement in transplant rates.

Dear Sir,

In response to your article - it is about time organ donation laws were changed. The opt-out system sounds like the perfect solution. I am a donor and I carry a card. I believe it is important to donate organs and save people's lives. I would never want to force someone into donating their organs against their will, though.

Under the current voluntary system, so many life-saving organs are wasted. But, under the opt-out system, people who want out would have to actively do something about it. Therefore, more organs will be donated every year. This will give more people a chance to have life-saving organ transplant operations.

I think the opt-out system is a great way to take pressure off the family, too. They will not have to make a decision on behalf of their dead loved one at a difficult time.

The current system obviously isn't working. It needs to be changed, and everyone wins with the opt-out system.

T.J. Singh, NSW

Dear Editor,

I was upset when I read your article. The idea of presuming that everyone wants to be a donor is terrible. There are many different reasons why people don't want to donate their organs. They should not have to justify these reasons to the government.

There is a lot of potential for the opt-out system to be abused. People could be pressured into donating. If they want to opt-out, they might be made to feel guilty for their decision. What if their opt-out form gets lost in the post? What if they don't get around to opting out before they die? People entering the opt-out information into the computer database could "accidentally" leave a person's details out.

I also think it is important that a patient's family members are shown compassion while they are grieving. They need to be involved in any decision about organ donation.

The best way to tackle the organ shortage is to educate people about the issue. Encourage more people to sign up to the current voluntary system.

A. Andrews, QLD

The ownership of your organs comes into question under a compulsory system.

Make It Completely Compulsory!

The opt-out policy proposed in your article is just a half measure. Too many people will opt out and the organ shortage problem will continue. Organ donation should be completely compulsory. Nobody should be able to opt out.

Look at it this way. If you were dying, I'm sure you'd accept the offer of another person's organs. It would save your life! So, why wouldn't you donate your organs after your death?

It's perfectly reasonable to make organ donation compulsory. There is too much emphasis placed on the sensitivities of donors and their families. There is not enough on the needs of people waiting for transplants to save their lives.

Too many organs are being wasted because people are being selfish. About 30 per cent of family members refuse to give permission for a patient's organs to be removed. While it is important to show grieving families compassion, it needs to be one rule for everybody. Compulsory organ donation is the only system that will put an end to the organ shortage problem.

If a person wants to object to being a donor, maybe they should visit someone who is waiting for an organ transplant. They can explain why they would want the person to die instead of having their organs.

Dr Cook, NT

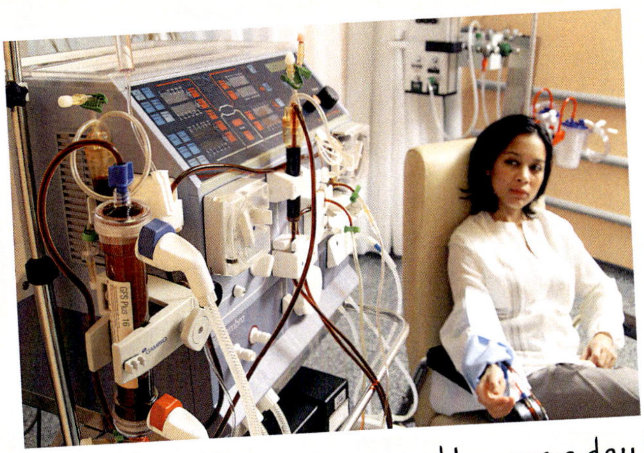

Many people have to spend several hours a day having their blood cleaned by a machine. Their only other option is to have a kidney transplant.

ASTHMA

Do you know what asthma is? Maybe someone in your class has it. You might even have it yourself.

Asthma is a type of breathlessness. It is a common condition that affects a person's airways and is caused by a partial blocking of the small bronchial tubes in the lungs. This makes it difficult for a person to get air in and out of their lungs.

An Asthma Attack

Asthma can affect a person in sudden attacks called asthma attacks. At first, the muscles that line the walls of the airways become inflamed and tighten. A person might feel this tightening sensation in their chest. Then, the mucus membranes that line the airways swell and produce thick mucus called phlegm. This causes the airways to narrow and the person begins to cough and wheeze. During an asthma attack, the person may gasp for air and feel that they are suffocating.

Causes of Asthma

There are many things that can cause an asthma attack. A person can suffer an attack if they come into contact with something they are allergic to, or that irritates their airways. This can be an ordinary substance, such as pollen, dust or some foods. Stress, illness or exercise can also start an asthma attack. Even a sudden change in the weather may bring on an attack.

Asthma attacks can happen at any time.

Sunflowers and other plants contain pollens that can trigger asthma attacks in some people.

Treating Asthma

There is no cure for asthma, but there are medicines available that work to relieve the symptoms. Most asthmatics use small devices called inhalers to pump medicine into their airways. Inhalers work by taking the medicine directly to the lungs where it is needed.

How an Inhaler Works

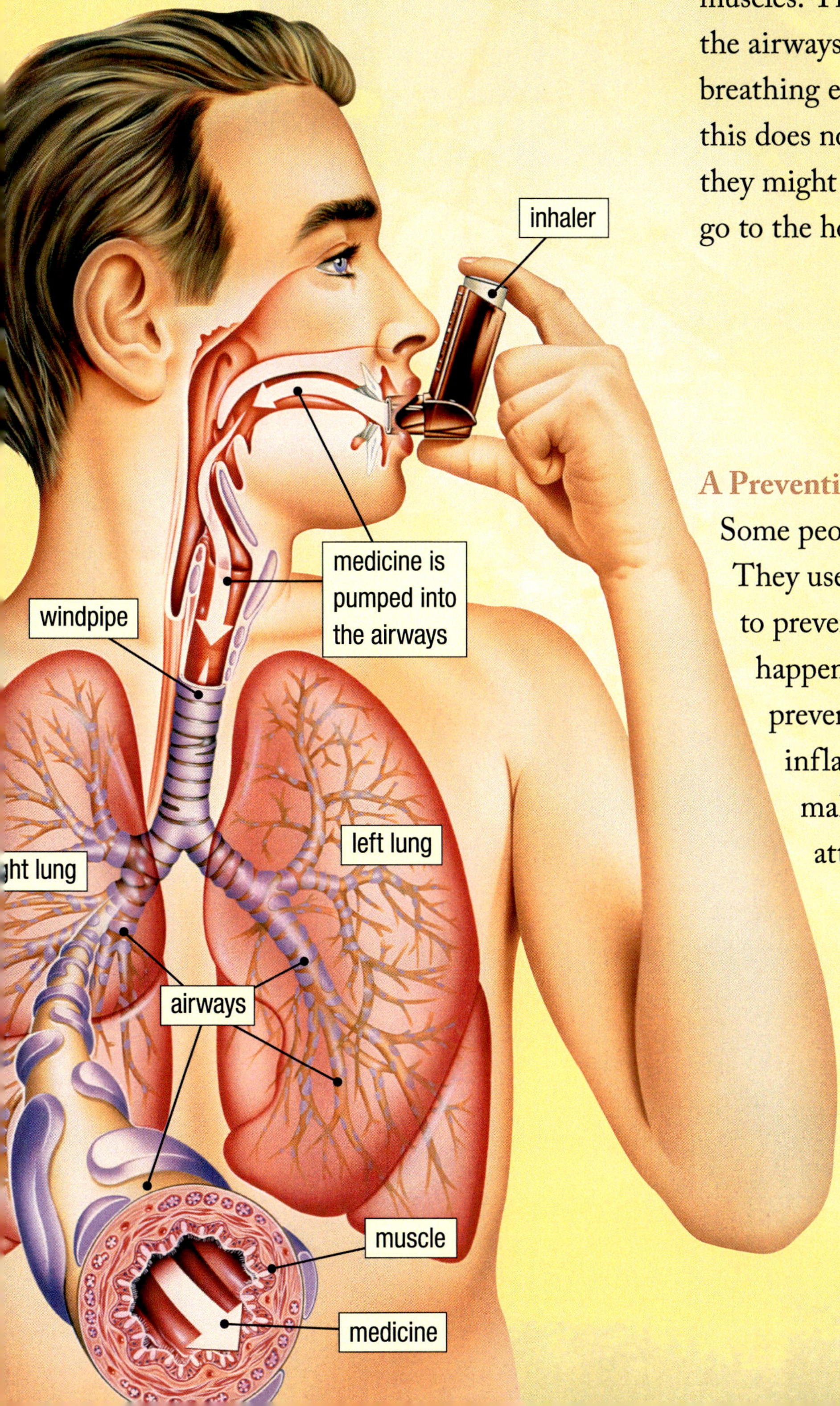

There are two main types of inhalers:

A Reliever Inhaler

A person can use a reliever inhaler during an attack. This pumps medicine into their airways to stop the attack. The medicine works quickly by relaxing the airway muscles. This opens the airways and makes breathing easier. If this does not work, they might need to go to the hospital.

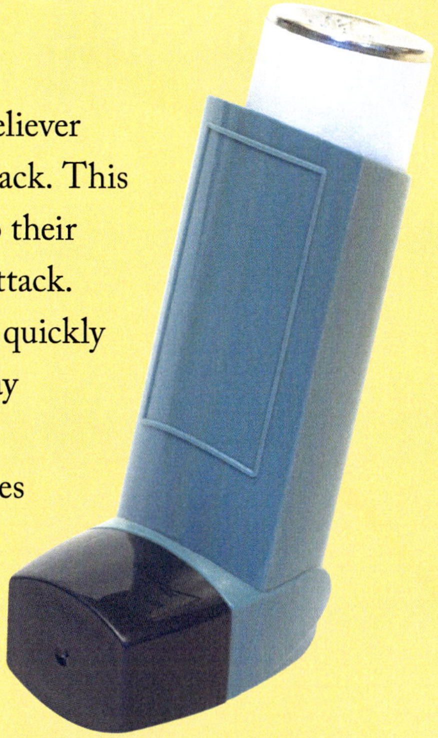

Inhalers can be used for prevention or relief of asthma attacks.

A Prevention Inhaler

Some people use a prevention inhaler. They use this inhaler every day to prevent an asthma attack from happening. The medicine in a prevention inhaler works by reducing inflammation in the lungs. This makes it less likely for an asthma attack to start.

Doctors can also prescribe other medications such as tablets, liquid medicines and injections if they need to.

An inhaler delivers medicine directly to where it is needed most.

ALLERGY VERSUS INTOLERANCE

Question:

My face swells and I get a rash when I eat peanuts. Do I have a food allergy or a food intolerance to peanuts? What is the difference?

Answer:

You probably have an allergy. Food allergies and food intolerances are both body reactions that occur in people who are sensitive to certain foods. However, they are very different.

If you think you might suffer from a food allergy or intolerance, a doctor should be able to answer your questions.

Food Allergies

An allergic reaction is caused by the body's immune system. A person's immune system protects them from infection. When they come into contact with harmful substances, such as bacteria or viruses, the immune system produces cells called antibodies to fight them. Sometimes, a person's immune system attacks harmless substances, too. When this happens, the reaction is called an allergy. When someone has a food allergy, their immune system reacts to the food as if it is not safe.

A substance that causes an allergy is called an allergen. There are many different allergens that can cause an allergic reaction. Any food can cause an allergic reaction, but some are more common than others. Foods such as eggs, shellfish and peanuts can cause allergic reactions. Other foods, such as tomatoes, celery, sesame seeds and milk can cause allergic reactions, too.

An allergy develops when the body comes into contact with an allergen more than once. The contact can be by touching, swallowing or breathing in the allergen. The body reacts by producing protective proteins called antibodies. The antibodies and allergen then act together to release chemical substances called H-substances into the person's blood. The most common H-substance is called histamine. This causes an allergic reaction such as coughing, sneezing, swelling, watering eyes or a rash. These symptoms appear quickly and can be mild or severe. If a person has a severe food allergy, it can cause a life-threatening reaction.

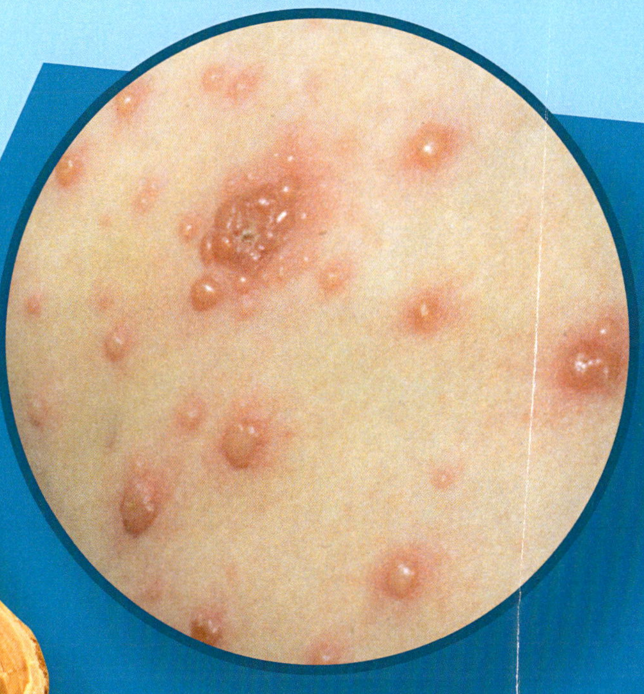

Allergic reactions may cause rashes or swelling of the skin, among other symptoms.

Many people suffer from allergies to substances such as peanuts.

There is no cure for an allergy. If possible, it is best to avoid the allergen that causes it. For example, do not eat peanuts if they cause a rash and swelling. Most minor allergies can be controlled with a medicine called antihistamine. This stops the body reacting to histamine in the blood. More severe allergies may be treated with steroids. Some allergies can be treated with injections. A small amount of the allergen is injected into the body regularly for a period of time. It is not enough to cause a reaction, but over time, the body gets used to the allergen and stops reacting to it.

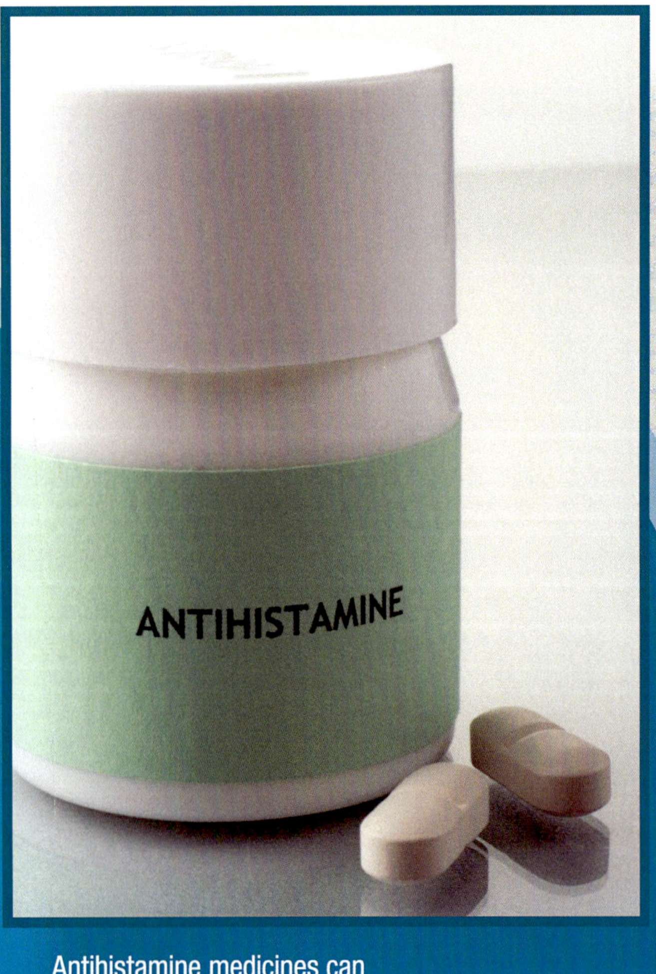

Antihistamine medicines can help stop the body reacting to histamines in the blood.

Food Intolerances

Food intolerances do not involve the immune system. It is the body's reaction to a food that it cannot break down, or digest. The body does not produce enough of the enzyme needed to digest the particular food. Therefore, the body rejects the food it cannot digest.

If a person eats a food they are intolerant to, they can feel ill. The undigested food passes through the person's intestines. It can cause discomfort or pain. They may suffer from stomach cramps, nausea or diarrhoea. Parts of the undigested food can even damage the intestines. Unlike an allergy, these symptoms may occur some time after the food is eaten. Two of the most common food intolerances are caused by foods that contain milk and wheat products.

Dairy and wheat are two of the most common foods that can cause food intolerance.

While food intolerances are not life threatening, they can cause a lack of nutrients in the body. This is because the body fails to absorb the nutrients from the particular food. For example, people who have intolerance to milk may get very little calcium. This can weaken their bones. Over time, food intolerance can cause a person to become unhealthy.

The best treatment for food intolerance is to avoid eating the food that causes it. To detect food intolerance, a person can go on a controlled diet. They can stop eating the food they think is causing the intolerance. Once the symptoms go, they can then eat the food again. If the symptoms return, the intolerance is confirmed and the food should be avoided.

Allergies and food intolerances can both affect a person's health. Therefore, it is important that they are identified and treated.

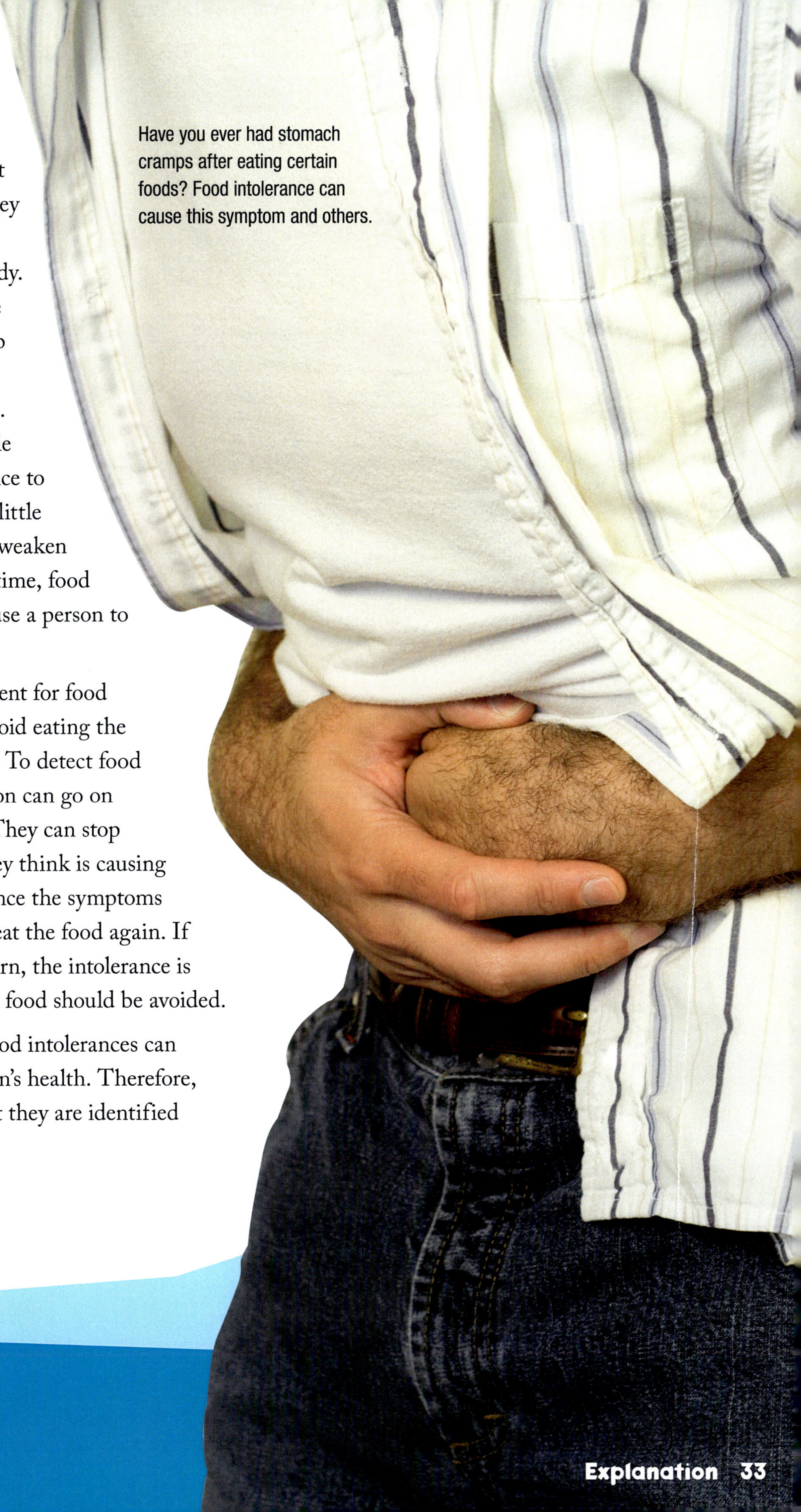

Have you ever had stomach cramps after eating certain foods? Food intolerance can cause this symptom and others.

A-Choo!

Substances that seem harmless wreak havoc with people all over the world every day. They send many people into a frenzy of sneezing, scratching, swelling and other reactions. Why? Because many substances trigger allergic reactions.

Allergic reactions are caused by the body's immune system reacting as if a substance is harmful. There are many allergens that can cause reactions. These include dust, pollen and mould spores. Food products that contain gluten and grains can also cause allergic reactions. Some people are allergic to chemicals in soaps and cleaning products. Clothing made from wool and leather can also cause allergic reactions in some people.

People suffer different reactions to these allergens. Some symptoms are mild, such as sneezing or watery eyes. These symptoms are merely irritating for the person suffering. They are not usually life-threatening. However, some people can suffer more severe reactions. They could have difficulty breathing or become unconscious. These reactions can be life threatening.

One of the most common allergic reactions is called hay fever. It is mostly caused by pollen from trees, flowers, grasses and weeds. It usually affects people in spring and summer. The most common symptoms of hay fever are sore, watery eyes, sneezing and sinus congestion. In some people, hay fever can lead to breathing problems and itchy skin.

Other allergens can also cause similar symptoms to hay fever. These allergens include mould spores, dust and animal skin or feathers.

Some allergens can cause severe reactions. These reactions include swelling and a severe rash. Sometimes, they can make people unconscious, or even kill them. Some chemicals, such as latex rubber and antibiotics, can also cause severe allergic reactions. Some food allergies, such as peanuts, eggs and tree nuts, are another cause of severe allergic reactions. People who suffer severe allergic reactions must be very careful to avoid the allergen. People can take drugs to manage the symptoms, or they can try to avoid the allergen altogether.

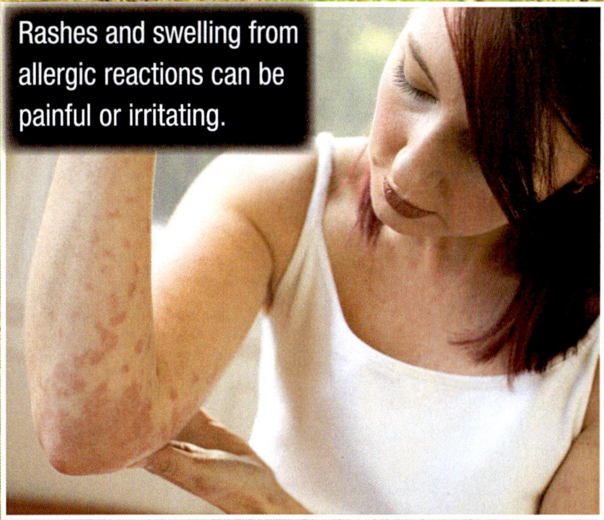
Rashes and swelling from allergic reactions can be painful or irritating.

This child has a swollen eye, which can be a symptom of an allergic reaction.

Anaphylactic SHOCK

Some people have mild reactions to allergens. But, some people have severe life-threatening reactions.

One kind of severe allergic reaction is called anaphylactic shock. It affects a person's whole body and can be life threatening if it is not treated immediately. Anaphylactic shock is triggered the same way as other allergies. A person's immune system overreacts to an allergen. This causes large quantities of histamine and other substances to be released into the person's blood. This can lead to a sudden drop in the person's blood pressure and rapid swelling that can block the person's airways. It is very dangerous and can be fatal!

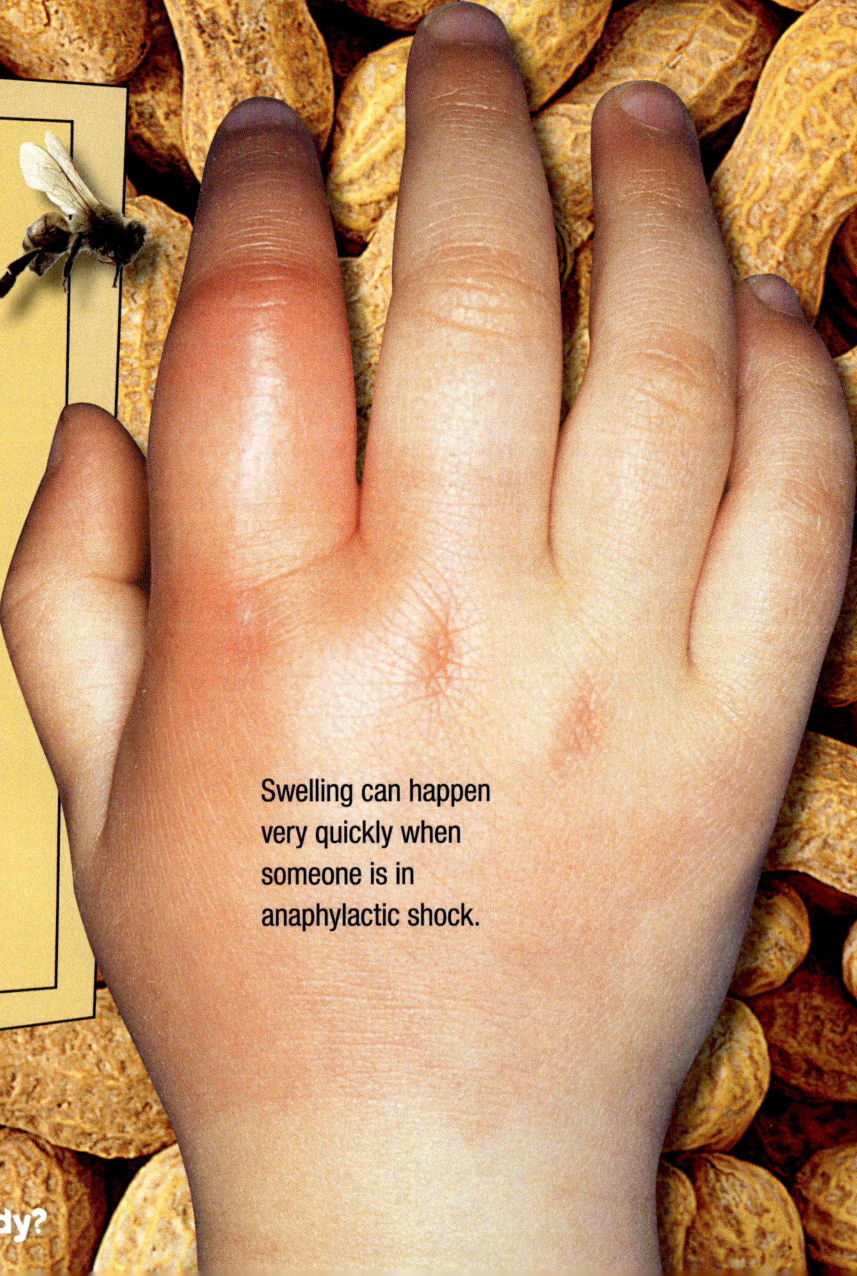

Swelling can happen very quickly when someone is in anaphylactic shock.

A person can suffer an anaphylactic reaction by eating, touching or smelling an allergen. The reaction can occur in response to any allergen. The most common causes of anaphylactic shock include medications, natural latex rubber and venom from bee and wasp stings. Foods such as peanuts, shellfish and eggs are also common allergens that can cause anaphylactic shock.

Common allergens include shellfish, eggs and nuts, among other things.

A person who is severely allergic to something may suddenly feel very unwell.

Anaphylactic shock generally causes a whole body reaction. Therefore, it can cause many symptoms. These symptoms can include itchy lumps on a person's skin. These are called hives. The person's chest can tighten and they can wheeze as they have difficulty breathing. Nausea, stomach cramps and vomiting are also common symptoms. As the histamine lowers the person's blood pressure, the person's body goes into shock. This can cause the person to collapse. Swelling can block the person's airways so they cannot breathe. This can damage the person's brain and other organs.

If a person suffers anaphylactic shock, they need medical treatment immediately. Doctors usually treat anaphylactic shock with a drug called epinephrine. Epinephrine helps to open the person's airways and stimulate their heart to continue beating. This can be given through a syringe called an EpiPen. Doctors may also use oxygen to help restore the person's blood pressure and breathing.

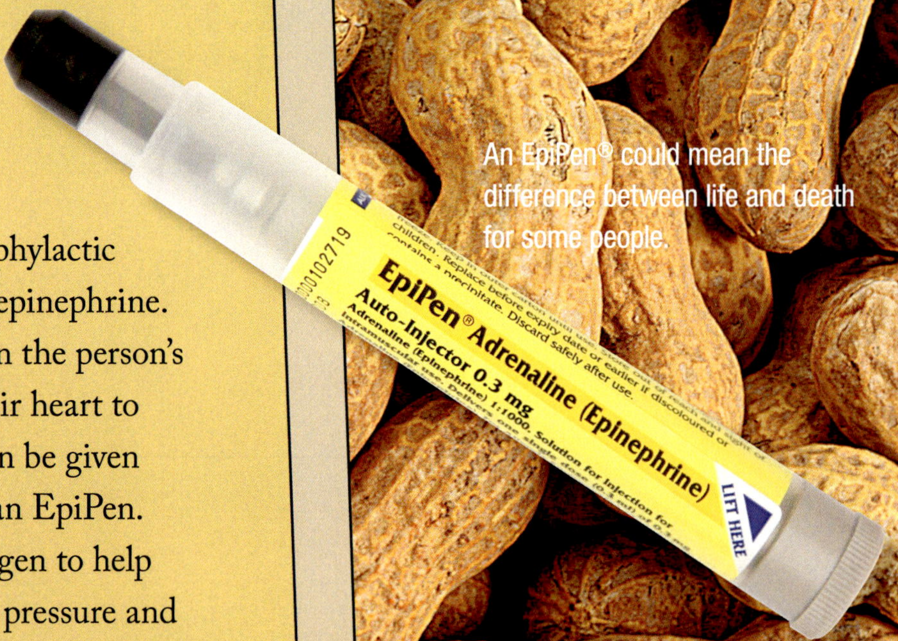

An EpiPen® could mean the difference between life and death for some people.

If a person has serious allergies, they should try to protect themselves against anaphylactic shock. First, they should find out what it is that they are allergic to. Then, they should try to keep away from the allergen. Because an anaphylactic reaction often occurs quickly, it is usually simple to identify the allergen that caused the attack. If there is any doubt, a doctor can carry out blood and skin tests on a person to identify the allergen.

If a person knows they have severe allergies, they can wear a medical bracelet that lists the allergens that can cause an anaphylactic attack. They can carry an emergency EpiPen® to use if they have an attack. These simple steps could mean the difference between life and death!

Some people wear medical bracelets like this one, so that others know they have an allergy.

I am allergic to peanuts. If I eat or touch anything that has peanuts in it, I will have an anaphylactic reaction. I have to be very careful because there are many food products that contain peanuts or traces of peanuts. I make sure I read the labels of all food products.

Our home is a peanut-free zone! My parents thought about home schooling me so I didn't risk an attack at school. In the end we decided the best plan was for me to be careful and prepared. So, at school, I try to avoid children who have peanuts or peanut products in their lunch. I wear a medical bracelet to let people know I'm allergic to peanuts. I also have an emergency plan. It outlines the steps people should take if I have an anaphylactic attack. I have given a copy to my school and my netball coach.

I make sure that I always carry an EpiPen®. If I start to have an attack, I need to inject myself. This will hopefully relieve the symptoms until I get to a hospital. I keep a spare EpiPen® at school, too.

Allergies can be very serious. It is important that if you know someone has a severe allergy, you take care to keep the allergen away.

People who suffer from allergies can still lead normal lives.

Get with the Beat

When you exercise, your muscles move parts of your bone structure, or skeleton. This requires a lot of energy! Your blood carries oxygen to the cells in your muscles to make the energy. When you exercise, your heart pumps faster to pump more oxygenated blood to your hard-working muscles. You can feel your heart pump faster by checking your pulse rate.

To complete this task, work with a partner. You will need a digital stopwatch or an analogue watch with a second hand.

Step 1. Find Your Pulse

You can check your pulse at your wrist or at your neck.

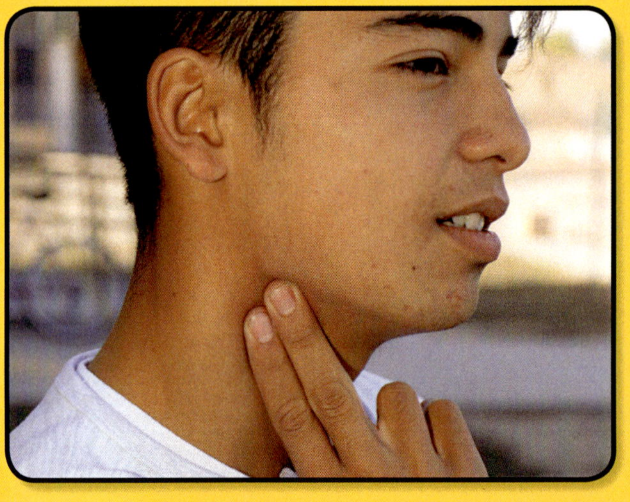

To measure your pulse at your neck:

1. Place your index and middle fingers in the soft hollow at the side of your neck, close to your voice box.
2. Keep your fingers flat and press firmly until you feel your pulse.

To measure your pulse at your wrist:

1. Use your index and middle fingers of your right hand.
2. Place these fingers over the underside of your left wrist.
3. Keep your fingers flat and press firmly until you feel your pulse.

Step 2. Check Your Resting Pulse Rate

This is your pulse rate when you are at rest. Most people have a resting pulse rate of between 60–100 beats per minute.

1. Find your pulse at your wrist or at your neck.

2. Ask your partner to start timing. Count the beats for 30 seconds.

3. Multiply the number of beats by two.

4. Write down this number. This is your pulse rate in beats per minute.

Step 3. Check Your Pulse Rate After Exercise

1. Ask your partner to time you.

2. Jog on the spot for two minutes.

3. Take your pulse for 30 seconds.

4. Multiply this number by two.

5. Write down this number.

Now, swap places with your partner and assist them to complete steps 1–3.

Step 4. Check Your Resting Pulse Rate Again

When your partner has completed steps 1–3, check your resting pulse rate again. Write down this number. Then, assist your partner to do the same.

Answer these questions:

Is your resting pulse rate the same as it was at step 2?

Were your pulse rates the same as your partner's?

Step 5. Record your Results

Recording your results will help you to make conclusions about your fitness. People often have different pulse rates. A person who plays a lot of sport might find their pulse rate is different to a person who does not do a lot of activity.

In groups of six to eight students, prepare a table. It needs to show:

1. The number of hours of sport or training each student does per week.

2. Their resting pulse rate.

3. Their pulse rate after exercise.

What conclusions can you make from the information in the table?

Mad about Health

By Michael Rosen

A rap is a kind of rhyming word play, normally spoken over a beat. This excerpt from a rap is about someone who is crazy about his health. Can you have too much of a good thing?

I eat carrots
I eat cabbage
I eat sprouts
I eat radish

look after myself
I'm mad about health
mad about health
mad about myself

don't eat sugar
don't eat fat
what about salt?
don't eat that

I go for a jog
I go for a swim
I go for a run
I go to the gym[...]

feel my pulse rate
feel my biceps
feel my kneecap
feel my triceps
I'm really fit
but d'you know what?
my right knee
hurts a lot.

look after myself
I'm mad about health
mad about health
mad about myself

right knee's swollen
ankle's sprained
wrist is twisted
shoulder's strained

but I'm really fit
I'm much stronger
never mind the pain
I'm gonna live longer
something funny
I've been told
why work so hard
just to get old?

I don't get that
not at all
can't stop now
gotta do some more

look after myself
I'm mad about health
mad about health
mad about myself[...]

Mighty Marvel Muscle Meter

Want to improve your body?

Want to attract new friends?

Want to feel great?

Want to become superfit?

Try our new system and you will improve your body, attract new friends, feel great and become superfit!

Try the Mighty Marvel Muscle Meter

This amazing machine measures the benefits of your training. It gives you continuous feedback about how your muscles are reacting to exercise. By using this information, you can adjust your workout so your muscles get the maximum benefit from your exercise routine.

We guarantee it is better than any other system!

Well-known body builders and supermodels recommend it.

It is used more than any other system by leading personal trainers and fitness instructors.

Over 75 per cent of people have said their muscle strength improved in just a few weeks.

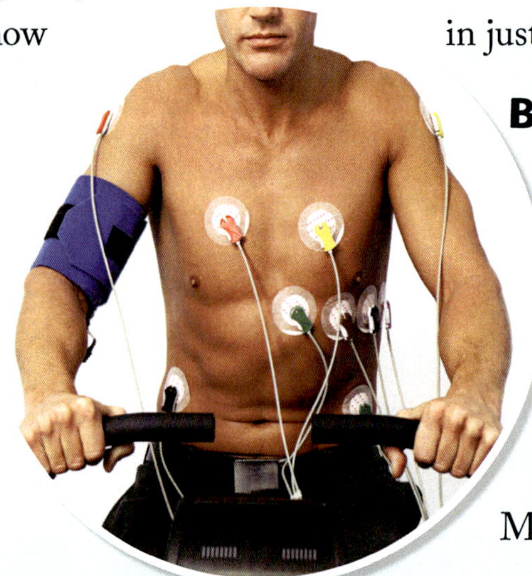

Buy Now!

If you don't get amazing results within 30 days, we'll refund your money.

Phone Tony on 363 362 to find out the incredibly low price of the Mighty Marvel Muscle Meter.

Dear Editor,

I noticed an advertisement for a Mighty Marvel Muscle Meter in a recent copy of your magazine. I am concerned about the outrageous claims made by the advertisers. They can't guarantee that any of their claims will happen if a person uses their machine. In addition, I am appalled by their claim that it could help people attract new friends. I would also like to know – who are the body builders and supermodels that have recommended this product? I notice that the advertiser doesn't provide any names.

I am shocked that your magazine printed this advertisement. Surely there are laws against such advertisements being printed and it doesn't add to your magazine's reputation. I would be interested to see you print your advertising guidelines and rules in your next issue to show what kind of advertising is permitted in your magazine.

J. Smythe

Dear Editor,

I am concerned about the advertisement that appeared in your magazine for the Mighty Marvel Muscle Meter. I am a personal trainer and I do not know of any machine that could provide the kind of results promised by the advertisers

Therefore, their claim that it is 'better than any other system' is redundant, as there isn't another system similar to this on the market. Even if there was, I fail to see of what use the information recorded by the machine would be to a person's fitness routine.

For most people, the best way to improve their fitness is to remember a simple phrase – move more. If a person takes every opportunity to walk instead of drive, use stairs instead of a lift, choose outdoor activities over sitting in front of televisions and computers, the fitness of our community would increase markedly. People don't need fancy gadgets and gizmos; they just need to move.

M. Faban

Funtastic Human Body

Please do not write on these pages. The activities are reproduced as photocopiable pages in the Literacy Network Upper Primary Teacher Resource Book. The answers can also be found in the Teacher Resource Book.

1. Invisible Activity

Use the clues below to complete the puzzle and identify parts of the body that we rarely see working. Use the letters that you write in the shaded parts of the grid to name a major process of the human body.

1. Another name for a person's windpipe
2. A large organ in a person's abdomen
3. An organ that works like a pump
4. Tissue that moves your bones
5. These organs are used for breathing
6. The smallest blood vessels in the body
7. An organ in which part of digestion occurs
8. A person's bone structure
9. Central part of the nervous system
10. The red liquid pumped around the body
11. Carry impulses from brain to parts of body

2. Left Overs

Cross out each instance of the letters that appear more than once. Then use the remaining letters to discover the name of one of the major systems of the body. Note: you will need to rearrange the letters to get the correct answer.

A F N O R V L M S B

B C A E P I M A C L

B M I B F U H L H P

_ _ _ _ _ _ _ _ system

Did You Know?

A drop of blood the size of a pinhead contains about five million red blood cells!

3. Drastic Results

Amy cannot eat eggs. Use the hour time code below to find out what she might suffer if she ate an egg sandwich.

12.00 10.00 12.00 8.00 2.00 4.00 3.00 12.00 7.00 6.00 5.00 7.00 1.00 2.00 9.00 7.00 11.00

Joke Corner:

Q: What vessels never sail?

A: Blood vessels

Q: What did the cardiologist say when he examined the athlete's heart?

A: Beaten again!

Create and share some of your own jokes about the human body.

4. Major Operation

Use the grid and the coordinates to help Dr Ranstein discover what his first operation for the day will be.

	1	2	3	4
5	L	S	E	U
6	N	H	R	G
7	A	P	T	D

Coordinates

6,2 5,3 7,1 6,3 7,3 7,1 6,1 7,4 5,1 5,4 6,1 6,4

7,3 6,3 7,1 6,1 5,2 7,2 5,1 7,1 6,1 7,3

5. Allergy Tower

Rearrange the letters on each level of the tower to identify some common allergens. The letters in the shaded boxes are the first letters of each word.

g s **e** g

l k i **m**

d s t u

s r a s **g**

a **g** i r n

l o l **p** n e

t a o m o **t**

l e **g** n u t

a u **p** s n t e

h f l s i e h l **s**